Close to the Wind

Haiku North America Anthologies

Harvest (1991)
The Shortest Distance (1993)
Northern Lights (1995)
Shades of Green (1997)
Too Busy for Spring (1999)
Paperclips (2001)
Brocade of Leaves (2003)
Tracing the Fern (2005)
Dandelion Wind (2007)
Into Our Words (2009)
Standing Still (2011)
Close to the Wind (2013)

Close to the Wind

*An anthology of poems
commemorating the 2013
Haiku North America conference*

Michael Dylan Welch
and William Hart, *Editors*

Naia, *Illustrations*

PRESS HERE
Sammamish, Washington

PRESS HERE
22230 NE 28th Place
Sammamish, Washington
98074-6408 USA

ISBN 978-1-878798-35-0

First printing, August 2013

Copyright © 2013 by Michael D. Welch

All rights revert to the authors upon publication in this book. No part of this book may be used or reproduced in any manner whatsoever without written permission from the contributor except in the case of brief quotations in reviews.

This book is a commemorative anthology of poems by attendees and participants in Haiku North America 2013, an international celebration of haiku and related genres of poetry held aboard the Queen Mary in Long Beach, California from August 14 through 18, 2013. Each attendee who chose to submit poems was guaranteed to have one selected for inclusion in this anthology.

Cover art and illustrations by Naia.
Design and typography by Michael Dylan Welch.
Poems and names set in 14/20 Myriad Pro Semibold and
12/16 Myriad Pro Italic, with headings set in 20/22 Myriad Pro Bold.

www.haikunorthamerica.com

Out of the Harbor

Haiku, as Marlene Mountain once said, is not a port in a storm. And as seafarers know, sailing close to the wind means traveling into the wind as directly as one possibly can. This makes for difficult and even dangerous sailing, but facing the wind is sometimes absolutely necessary. As the English-language haiku community navigates various swells and sea changes, including the influence of gendai haiku and reactions for and against it, perhaps we might all be sailing close to the wind. The good news is that, at least for the long weekend of the 2013 Haiku North America conference in Long Beach, California, our crew is all safely docked in the harbor, sharing its poems and viewpoints. But who knows which way we'll each be sailing next?

The location of this year's conference aboard the Queen Mary ocean liner naturally lends itself to a nautical theme. Naia's illustrations for this collection of haiku and senryu by conference attendees have extended this theme to explore seaside subjects. Some say the old ship that hosts our conference is haunted. Even if not, the Queen Mary's wooden decks and elegant staterooms carry much history and tradition. It's from such a solid grounding in the past that we can set sail into the future. The HNA conference is indeed all about looking back as well as forward.

We hope you enjoy reading the poems in this anthology, our second largest in more than twenty years of biennial HNA conferences. As with all previous anthologies, we've arranged the poems by each poet's first name. Even when gales are lashing and we're sailing close to the wind, here's hoping we can maintain our close-knit spirit of community and always remain on a first-name basis.

Michael Dylan Welch
and William Hart, Editors

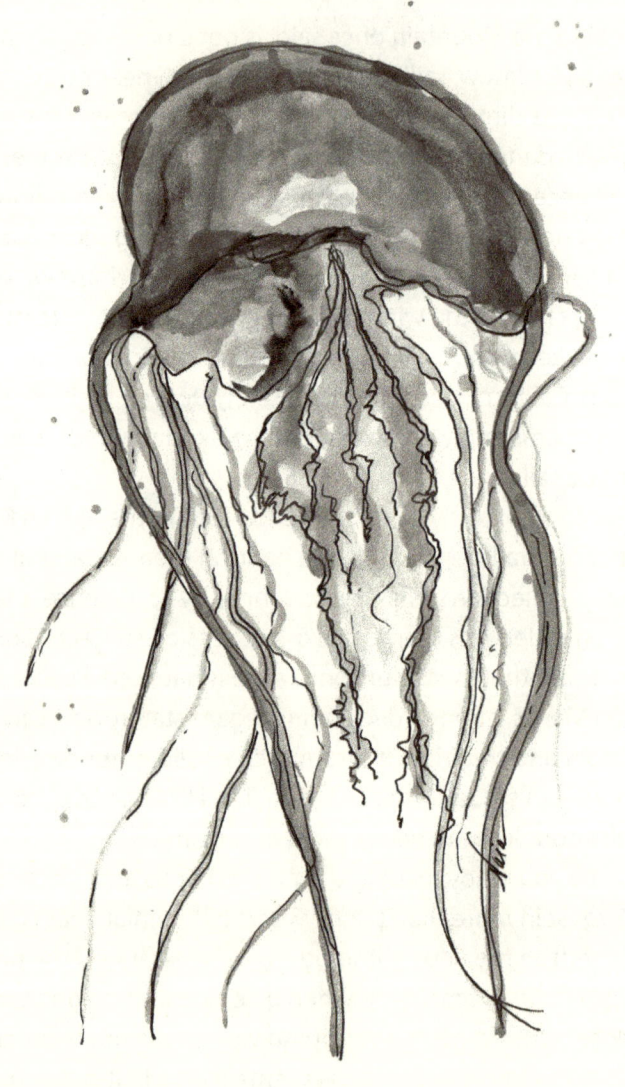

Bach cello
swallows sky mind
evening splinters

> Ambika Talwar
> Los Angeles, California

this morning
angel wings
on the rooftop

> Andrea Eldridge
> Claremont, California

the river fills with stars . . .
we always thought
we would have tomorrow

> Angela Terry
> Lake Forest Park, Washington

a spider strand
catches the last of the sun
the clamor of mynahs

> Angelee Deodhar
> Chandigarh, India

our wedding rings
in the velvet box—
forked roads

> Anita Curran Guenin
> San Diego, California

perfectly pawdicured pet with mismatched socks

> Anna Kondo
> Atlanta, Georgia

Oklahoma kids
buried alive in rubble
their last day of school

> Barbara Hay
> Ponca City, Oklahoma

summer dusk—
sunset and moonrise
in one breath

> Beki Reese
> Costa Mesa, California

Bohemian waxwings—
and I didn't even have
a bucket list

> Billie Wilson
> Juneau, Alaska

a few petals
left by the sweeper . . .
sunset clouds

> Bill Kenney
> Whitestone, New York

midnight train
even the transient
keeps up appearances

> Brosnan Rhodes
> Los Angeles, California

after heart surgery
they finish the mandala
jigsaw puzzle

> Bruce H. Feingold
> Berkeley, California

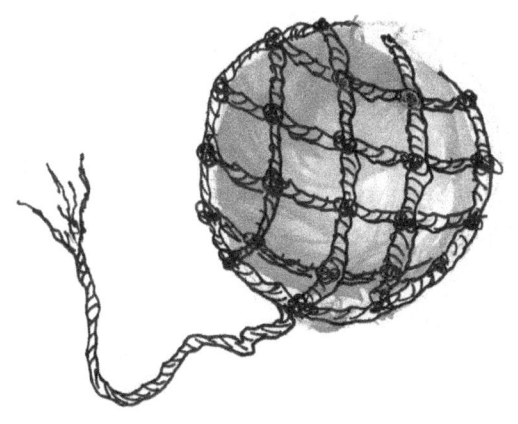

Muir Woods . . .
stepping into
his words

> Carol Judkins
> Carlsbad, California

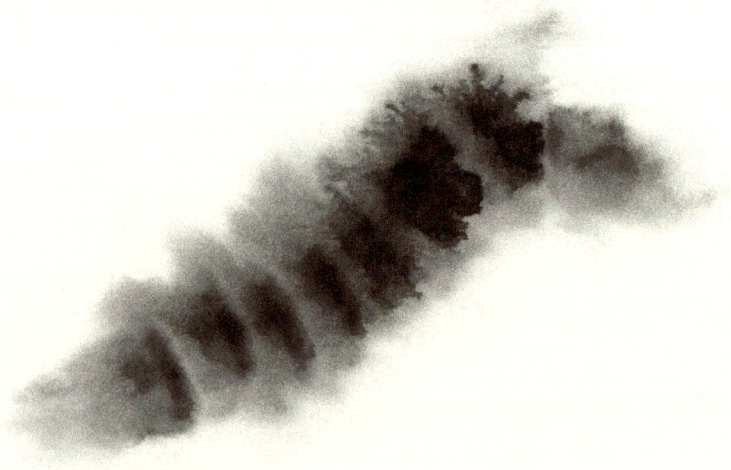

**Googling
the (OMG venomous!) centipede
in my hand**

> Carolyn Hall
> San Francisco, California

she drones on
about writing from the heart
the hard conference chairs

>   *Charles Trumbull*
>   *Santa Fe, New Mexico*

rolling hills—
wheat pennies in the jar
on my father's desk

>   *Cherie Hunter Day*
>   *Cupertino, California*

**threadbare
in the knot
my emergency tie**

> *David G. Lanoue*
> *New Orleans, Louisiana*

**Rubbing words, like silk,
between my fingers. Smooth, soft,
stronger than they look.**

> *Deborah Edler Brown*
> *Los Angeles, California*

**home again
after a week on the road
plum blossoms**

> *Deborah P Kolodji*
> *Temple City, California*

summer moon—
out of darkness
a leaf

> Diana Ming Jeong
> Pasadena, California

the rock
thinking about rolling,
rolling . . .

> Don Baird
> Palmdale, California

after sunset
  sometimes the clouds light up
let's wait and see

  Don Eulert
  Santa Ysabel, California

prison concert—
the harpist peering out
through the strings

> Don McLeod
> Sherman Oaks, California

rust on my driveway
blends with HOA hues
yet I get letters

> Elizabeth Williams
> San Luis Rey, California

wet sand—
the stork's legs
twice as long

> Ellen Cooper
> Montréal, Québec

at the edge of the sea entering the barely there

Eve Luckring
Los Angeles, California

summer stars
a travel-sized
Aladdin's Lamp

Fay Aoyagi
San Francisco, California

a dry spring breeze
shakes the old yucca flowers—
rain on my roof

Frank C. Carey
Santa Fe, New Mexico

**Tin sunset
the toy robot
walks off the table**

*Garry Gay
Santa Rosa, California*

**facing the wind
fading words
on the sign**

Gary Hotham
Scaggsville, Maryland

**the potato peeler on the table
pointing to him—
life is sometimes quiet**

Gene Myers
Rockaway, New Jersey

raw oysters
she remembers
her first time

    Genie Nakano
    Hawthorne, California

in pine shade
a mother and daughter talk
Boy Scout camp

    Gregory Longenecker
    Pasadena, California

Graceland
50 shades
of Elvis

    Haiku Elvis (Carlos W. Colón)
    Shreveport, Louisiana

**no alarm
feathered friends
breaking fast**

*James Won
Temple City, California*

**jacaranda petals
stain the sidewalk
first love**

*Janis Albright Lukstein
Rancho Palos Verdes, California*

**dry riverbed
too late to say
sorry**

*Jennifer Sutherland
Glen Waverley, Australia*

pink buds of crab apple tree
as big as the later fruit

> Jim Applegate
> Roswell, New Mexico

the crickets stop chirping that much dawn

> Jim Kacian
> Winchester, Virginia

**autumn chill
dialing her dead mother's number
by mistake**

> Joan Prefontaine
> Cottonwood, Arizona

snow has made a coffin of a stone bench

> John Stevenson
> Nassau, New York

**lotus buds
the glint of pennies
in the fountain**

> Joshua Gage
> Cleveland, Ohio

composted key
does it open a world
on the other side

Kath Abela Wilson
Pasadena, California

produce aisle
a child listens
to the melons

Kathe L. Palka
Flemington, New Jersey

**white sea foam
abandoned at high tide
stretch marks**

> *Kathy Fulton*
> *Westminster, California*

**testing the hotness
of the iron
    spring rain**

> *Kimberly Esser*
> *Los Angeles, California*

they can tie the knot
after all
those years in the closet

  kris moon
  Kanagawa, Japan

in my dream
I touch the moon
and it is real

  Lidia Rozmus
  Vernon Hills, Illinois

beach house—
the scent of sunscreen
in an unmade bed

  Linda M. Papanicolaou
  Palo Alto, California

piano fugue—
Glen Gould's
twenty fingers

> Luce Pelletier
> St. Basile le Grand, Québec

summer moonlight . . .
stretching the strings
of a violin

> Makoto Nakanishi
> Matsuyama, Japan

after the divorce
she shoots his heirloom china
with his heirloom gun

> Marcyn Clements
> Claremont, California

clouds,
where there is no mountain
a mountain

> Margaret Beverland
> Katikati, New Zealand

branding time
the sun-tanned 'V'
on the cowhand's neck

> Margaret Chula
> Portland, Oregon

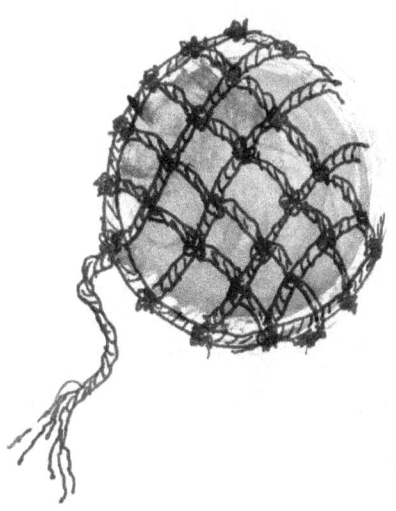

in Aoyama
an avenue of cherry trees
the other world

> Mariko Kitakubo
> Tokyo, Japan

another test
for glaucoma
I steal a magazine

> Marilyn Shoemaker Hazelton
> Allentown, Pennsylvania

a hand sticking out
from the balcony below . . .
small rain

    Michael Dylan Welch
    Sammamish, Washington

where other trees
reach upwards
the willow

    Michael Rehling
    Presque Isle, Michigan

a deer path peters
out in the periwinkle
morning moonset

    Michele Root-Bernstein
    East Lansing, Michigan

buoy bells . . .
her plan to forget one man
with another

> Naia
> Temecula, California

**maple leaf
fan
summer breeze**

> N. E. Taylor
> Los Angeles, California

massaging the dog eyes closed

> Oleg Kagan
> Los Angeles, California

**arriving late—
the others' footprints
snow-filled**

> Pamela Cooper
> Montréal, Québec

**frost-covered car
now some drama
in my life**

*Patrick Gallagher
San Francisco, California*

**windfall apple
a few geese that should
have moved on**

*paul m.
Bristol, Rhode Island*

**new grass
three horses shimmy
in the sand wallow**

>   *Paul MacNeil*
>   *Ocala, Florida*

**holiday cards
the connections that survive
those that don't**

>   *Peggy Heinrich*
>   *Santa Cruz, California*

**so sweet, this
unripe plum warmed
by your hand**

>   *Penny Harter*
>   *Mays Landing, New Jersey*

old year, new year
somewhere a hospital call bell
beeping and beeping

> pjm
> San Jose, California

at sunset memory feathers weighed against a cheek

> Richard Gilbert
> Kumamoto, Japan

winter of divorce
my son pulls apart
the fake white tree

> Roberta Beary
> Bethesda, Maryland

cheap highway motel
voice of the semi
penetrating rock and wall

    Robert Forsythe
    Annandale, Virginia

an emerald lagoon
colorful fish swim around
eating each other

    Robert Lundy
    Del Mar, California

distant party
a bush moth's wings beat
on the porch light

> Ron C. Moss
> Leslie Vale, Australia

wind from the south
her finger traces the character
for snow

> Sandra Simpson
> Tauranga, New Zealand

old hunting knife—
in the blood groove a trickle
of pear juice

> Scott Mason
> Chappaqua, New York

**the living room
now looking less lived-in—
spring cleaning**

> Sean Carlton
> West Hollywood, California

**summer evening—
a slip of moonlight
between her thighs**

> Seretta Martin
> San Diego, California

**cello music
the hotel room
feels warmer**

> *Sheila Sondik*
> *Bellingham, Washington*

**cedar rain—
all the hope
in mother's chest**

> *Sondra J. Byrnes*
> *South Bend, Indiana*

**loneliness—
the coffee
lukewarm**

> *Stanford M. Forrester*
> *Windsor, Connecticut*

Sparrows flit by.
Even the sick child
 finds a smile.

> Steve Carter
> Menlo Park, California

wilderness trail
that one moment
I felt lost

> *Stevie Strang*
> *Laguna Niguel, California*

a moment of peace . . .
her children's distant
shouting

> *Stewart C. Baker*
> *Rancho Palos Verdes, California*

**curriculum vitae
the years
that went missing**

> Susan Antolin
> Walnut Creek, California

boys hoot their leaps into the blue placid

> Susan Diridoni
> Kensington, California

**fine champagne,
wine and words
are better sipped**

> Susan Galletti Campion
> Spring Valley, California

**almost within reach
from the open bus window
tempting persimmon**

> *Susan Rogers*
> *Los Angeles, California*

**a doe . . .
the path through the forest
in her eyes**

> *Ted van Zutphen*
> *Healdsburg, California*

**summer dream
the earring maker's hands
on my neck**

> *Terry Ann Carter*
> *Victoria, British Columbia*

**pelicans
　　with nobody in charge
shift into glide**

*Ute Jamrozy
San Diego, California*

**cloudy half moon
their last daughter
moves out**

*Victor P. Gendrano
Seal Beach, California*

**with all its body
side-to-side over sand dunes
the tongue of god**

> *Victor Ortiz*
> *San Pedro, California*

**sin after sin
I kill mosquitoes
during meditation**

> *Vuong Pham*
> *Brisbane, Australia*

**the trail switchbacks up
through the forest
slug's pace**

> *Wakako Miya Rollinger*
> *Topanga, California*

fall twilight
in the bungalow for rent
a vacuum sings

> William Hart
> Montrose, California

Budding cherry
let's forget the formalities
and get started

> Yu Chang
> Schenectady, New York

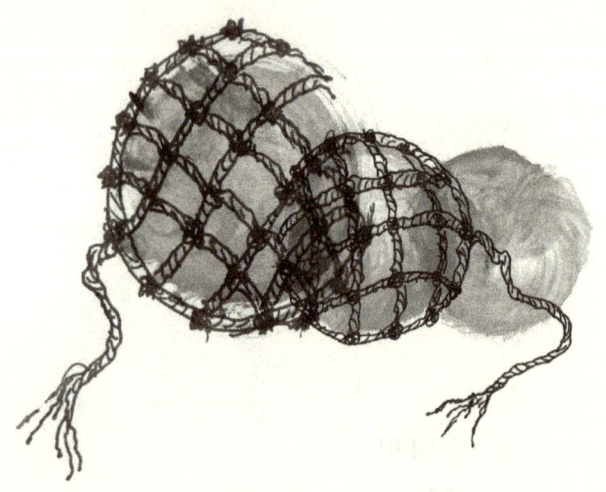

Contributors

Antolin, Susan 43	Forsythe, Robert 37
Aoyagi, Fay 18	Fulton, Kathy 26
Applegate, Jim 23	Gage, Joshua 24
Baird, Don 15	Gallagher, Patrick 34
Baker, Stewart C. 42	Gay, Garry 19
Beary, Roberta 36	Gendrano, Victor P. 45
Beverland, Margaret 29	Gilbert, Richard 36
Brown, Deborah Edler 14	Guenin, Anita Curran 9
Byrnes, Sondra J. 40	Haiku Elvis (Carlos W. Colón) . . . 21
Campion, Susan Galletti 43	Hall, Carolyn 12
Carey, Frank C. 18	Hart, William 5, 47
Carlton, Sean 39	Harter, Penny 35
Carter, Steve .41	Hay, Barbara 9
Carter, Terry Ann 44	Hazelton, Marilyn Shoemaker . . 30
Chang, Yu 47	Heinrich, Peggy 35
Chula, Margaret 29	Hotham, Gary 20
Clements, Marcyn 28	Jamrozy, Ute 45
Colón, Carlos W. (Haiku Elvis) 21	Jeong, Diana Ming 15
Cooper, Ellen 17	Judkins, Carol 12
Cooper, Pamela 33	Kacian, Jim 23
Day, Cherie Hunter 13	Kagan, Oleg 33
Deodhar, Angelee 8	Kenney, Bill 10
Diridoni, Susan 43	Kitakubo, Mariko 30
Eldridge, Andrea 7	Kolodji, Deborah P. 14
Elvis, Haiku (Carlos W. Colón) 21	Kondo, Anna 9
Esser, Kimberly 26	Lanoue, David G. 14
Eulert, Don 16	Longenecker, Gregory 21
Feingold, Bruce H. 11	Luckring, Eve 18
Forrester, Stanford M. 40	Lukstein, Janis Albright 22

Lundy, Robert 37
m., paul 34
Machmiller, Patricia J. (pjm) 36
MacNeil, Paul 35
Martin, Seretta 39
Mason, Scott 38
McLeod, Don 17
moon, kris 27
Moss, Ron C... 38
Myers, Gene 20
Naia 32
Nakanishi, Makoto. 28
Nakano, Genie 21
Ortiz, Victor 46
Palka, Kathe L. 25
Papanicolaou, Linda M. 27
Pelletier, Luce 28
Pham, Vuong 46
pjm (Patricia J. Machmiller) 36
Prefontaine, Joan 24
Reese, Beki 10

Rehling, Michael. 31
Rhodes, Brosnan 11
Rogers, Susan 44
Rollinger, Wakako Miya 46
Root-Bernstein, Michele 31
Rozmus, Lidia 27
Simpson, Sandra 38
Sondik, Sheila 40
Stevenson, John 24
Strang, Stevie 42
Sutherland, Jennifer 22
Talwar, Ambika 7
Taylor, N. E. 33
Terry, Angela 8
Trumbull, Charles. 13
van Zutphen, Ted 44
Welch, Michael Dylan 5, 31
Williams, Elizabeth. 17
Wilson, Billie. 10
Wilson, Kath Abela 25
Won, James 22

www.ingramcontent.com/pod-product-compliance
Lightning Source LLC
Chambersburg PA
CBHW051718040426
42446CB00008B/948